If Death Were A Woman

To Leslie,
Celebrate life!
Ellen

Poems by
Ellen Kort

Illustrations by
Jeffrey Hargreaves

Fox Print, Inc.
All Rights Reserved

Acknowledgements

If Death Were A Woman copyright (c) 1994 by Fox Print, Inc. All rights reserved. No portion of this book may be reproduced in any manner without written permission of Fox Print, Inc., except for excerpts contained in reviews or critical articles.

Published by Fox Print, Inc.
101 West Edison Avenue, Suite 247
Appleton, WI 54915
1-800-FOX-TALE (800-369-8253)

Poems by Ellen Kort
Illustrations by Jeffrey Hargreaves

ISBN 1-885520-03-4
Printed on recycled paper
First edition, 2,500 copies

Table of Contents

If Death Were A Woman 4

Small Pieces of Light 7

Counterclockwise 9

Instructions for Ashes..................................10

Cupped Against My Ear 13

To My Granddaughter's Future Lover 14

If Death Were A Woman

I'd want her to come for me
smelling of cinnamon   wearing
bright cotton   purple maybe   hot
pink   a red bandanna in her hair

She'd bring good coffee   papaya juice
bouquet of sea grass   saltine crackers
and a lottery ticket   We'd dip
our fingers into moist pouches

of lady-slippers   crouch down to see
how cabbages feel when wind bumps
against them in the garden
We'd walk through Martin's woods

find the old house   its crumbling
foundation strung with honeysuckle
and in the front yard   a surprise
jonquils   turning the air yellow

glistening and ripe   still blooming
for a gardener long gone   We'd head
for the beach   wearing strings of shells
around our left ankles   laugh

at their ticking sounds   the measured
beat that comes with dancing
on hard-packed sand   the applause
of ocean and gulls   She'd play

ocarina songs to a moon almost full
and I'd sing off-key   We'd glide
and swoop   become confetti of leaf fall
all wings   floating on small whirlwinds

never once dreading the heart-
silenced drop   And when it was time
she would not bathe me   Instead we'd
scrub the porch   pour leftover

water on flowers   stand a long time
in sun and silence   then   holding hands
we'd pose for pictures in the last light

Small Pieces Of Light

Stars have a way
of tightening the sky
offering small pieces
of light   A mother

tells her children
how on certain nights
moths refuse to come
to lanterns   fly

upward   fluttering
leaving dark imprints
against the full moon
A young girl pins

early morning laundry
on the clothesline
in the backyard
Somewhere a woman

has a rose tattooed
on pucker of skin
where her left breast
used to be   Tonight
here in this house
we inhale wet
breath of kitchen
slide crawfish into pot

of steaming water
They curl into red
fists   We place
each one on a platter

succulent flesh
carried like a prayer

Counterclockwise

Jars of raspberry jam   each
with a leaf of rose geranium
thinly paraffined on top
take us back to the dark warm
hug of bushes   so sweet

and heavy that for hours
after coming home we wear
ripeness on our hands
in our clothes   What is it
that opens a door or locks it
the eternal return
of memory   What circles
through the brain   in and out
of the heart   acid bite

of pin cherries   sweet fern
scent of vanilla   We gather
them all like windfall apples
press them through mill of time
let juices run   steam rise
into images   fragile as the one
moment we used to be sure of

Instructions For Ashes

I will trust you to give away
my turtle drum   rain stick
the redwood burl just beginning
to root   Return the borrowed books
old letters   hold me between thumb
and forefinger   Drop my ashes
dark as burnt paper   among chicory
alyssum   wild mint   Let me fall

like sunlight on irises unfolding
purple wings   Let me drop blueward
into sea   one salt crystal
in the shell's secret core   Feed me
to summer trout   Let the hounds
carry me home   through green gape
of morning   a burdock hooked
tight   riding the fine mesh

of fur   muscle and bone   falling
in farmyards   rising up in the cow's
small brown hills   crusted and dry
poked by a child's bare foot
Let me be welcome in folded leaves
cherry pit   appleseed   rose-
colored moon inside the grape
If there is to be a eulogy

let it be in the cloud of dust
coming up the road   a scar
in some poet's hand   Let it be
in riverbeds covered with snow
in the small talk of birds
clam-colored light
of early evening   Let it be one
last milkweed pod   spitting seeds

Cupped Against My Ear

I want sound of autumn leaf curl
that takes my breath like first

and sudden love   I want early frost
unnerving the garden   my mother's

pearl necklace against my throat
I want it all   dresses

whispering in closets   the slightest
lift of muslin curtain against

open window   September editing
dark purple trees   plum by falling plum

To My Granddaughter's Future Lover

Late some winter night   years from now
you may be the one to touch her cheek
her arm   the soft geometry where her body
ends and your hand begins   There may be
a low moon   snow   a murmur of owl
You may find comfort in the way her arm

covers your heart   the weight of your leg
over hers   Your breath may be warm
Your dreams may wander like stars
hurrying home   You may not know
that the future is something less
than a shrug of cells   the body's river

twisting through old tangled roots
that our worst losses are not in the past
but those directly ahead   You may not
yet know how kinship digs deeper
than any spring or cellar
is older than the green curve of seedfern

or the brightness in eyes   Yesterday
I made a drum   chiseled and sanded
the sounding edge   cut and soaked
goat skin   lacing it from top
to bottom   coming up from underneath
pulling it tight without tearing

When it dried and I thumbed it
for the first time   it was the same beat
her heart made when I held her
soon after she was born   how she nestled
against me   into my breast pouch
of warmth and sound

that timeless moment when what we gain
becomes equal to what we lose
and we enter   breathless
and unafraid   into our own perfect life

Ellen Kort, a winner of the Pablo Neruda Literary Prize for Poetry, is the author of 11 books and has been featured in a wide variety of journals and anthologies. Her poetry has been set to music and showcased as performance pieces in concert and on stage. She lives in Appleton, Wisconsin, and is Director of Writing Services for an advertising agency. She also presents poetry readings and Creative Writing, Inner Awareness and Mask-Making workshops throughout the United States, Australia, New Zealand and the Bahamas.

Jeffrey Hargreaves is an award-winning illustrator who also does murals and a wide variety of portraiture. He has served as an art instructor for elementary students and is convinced that his childhood drawings of whales with big teeth inspired him to explore the world of art. He is Creative Director for an advertising agency and makes his home in Appleton, Wisconsin, with his wife, a daughter, a son and a cat.